Prince

A Little Golden Book® Biography

By Nikki Shannon Smith

Illustrated by Don Tate

Golden Books
An imprint of Random House Children's Books
A division of Penguin Random House LLC
1745 Broadway, New York, NY 10019
penguinrandomhouse.com
rhcbooks.com

Library of Congress Control Number: 2024952916
ISBN 979-8-217-02545-9 (trade) — ISBN 979-8-217-02546-6 (ebook)
Manufactured in the United States of America
10 9 8 7 6 5 4 3 2 1
EU Contact: Penguin Random House Ireland, 32 Nassau Street, Dublin D02 YH68.
https://eu-contact.penguin.ie

On June 7, 1958, in Minneapolis, Minnesota, a baby was born. His father was not a king, and his mother was not a queen, but they named their baby Prince—Prince Rogers Nelson. The family didn't have much money, but Prince was born with an extraordinary gift. It was the gift of music, and he would soon share it with the world.

Prince's home was filled with music. His father was a hardworking songwriter and talented piano player, who played in a jazz band. Prince's mother sang in the band.

By the time he was three years old, Prince was already fascinated by his father's piano. He wanted to play, too, but he knew his dad's rule: Don't touch the piano.

When Prince was seven years old, his parents separated. It was a sad and difficult time for him, but without his father there, he was finally free to experiment with the piano. He taught himself to play the theme songs from television shows, like *Batman*.

Prince *had* to make music. He couldn't help it. Prince was just like his father.

Eventually, Prince's parents divorced, and he moved a lot. He lived with his mom, his dad, and his aunt. One thing didn't change though. Prince was always working on his music. At twelve years old, he could play several instruments, including drums and guitar. And when he moved into his friend André Cymone's basement, he had someone to play with.

In junior high school, Prince played baseball, football, and basketball, but he loved music more.

Early each morning, Prince practiced in the music room at school. He couldn't read music and wouldn't take lessons. Prince wanted the freedom to be creative. He played by ear, by heart, and by instinct. He was a natural, and people were beginning to notice.

In high school, Prince and André formed a band called Grand Central. They played other people's songs at school dances and parties. They were popular in Minneapolis, but Prince wanted to be popular everywhere. And he wanted to play his own music.

Prince recorded a demo tape, or sample, of his original songs. His unique sound combined rock, funk, punk, disco, jazz, and blues. Record companies liked what they heard and offered him deals. But Prince said no because they wouldn't let him produce his own music.

Prince was determined to bring people together with his blended style of music, so he played the songs in nightclubs instead.

Then something exciting happened. Prince's demo tape found its way to a concert promoter who thought Prince was as talented as Stevie Wonder. He helped Prince get a record deal with Warner Bros. It was the largest deal a new artist had ever been given, and Prince convinced the studio to let him produce his own music.

When he was only nineteen years old, Prince released his first record, *For You*. He played all *twenty-seven* instruments himself! Soon, he was invited to perform on a television show called *American Bandstand*.

The show's host, Dick Clark, asked Prince how many instruments he played. Prince smiled and shyly said a thousand.

Prince worked on new music day and night. In only four years, he released four more records.

He performed in colorful outfits made especially for him. He wore ruffles, high heels, makeup, and unique hairstyles. Prince leaped, twirled, and danced all over the stage. He described his band as a "rainbow" because the musicians had different skin tones, and there were both men and women.

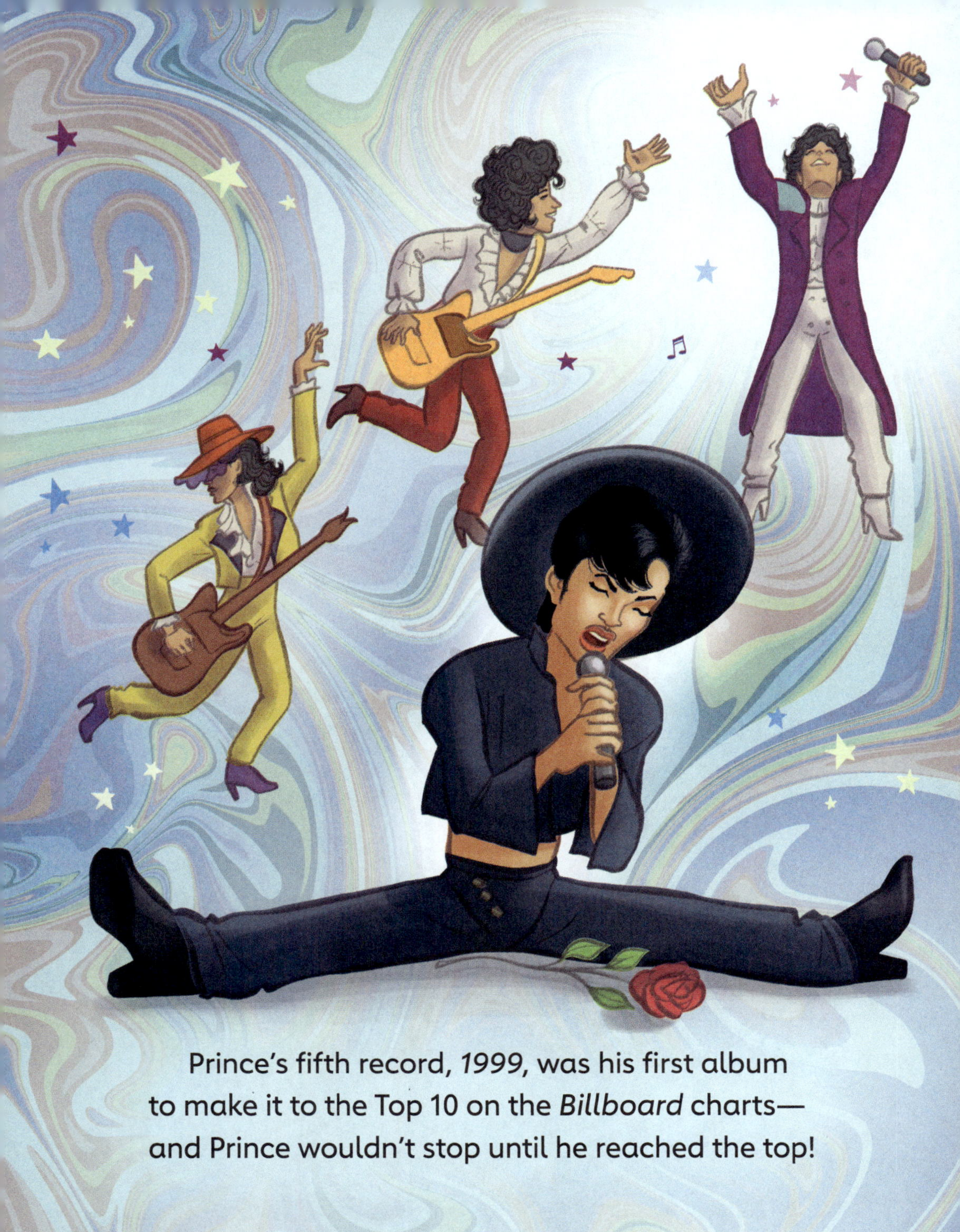

Prince's fifth record, *1999*, was his first album to make it to the Top 10 on the *Billboard* charts—and Prince wouldn't stop until he reached the top!

In 1984, Prince starred in a movie called *Purple Rain*. He also wrote nearly all the music for the movie—and people everywhere loved it. He won an Oscar and two Grammy Awards for the soundtrack. Prince was now more famous than ever.

He had a mansion built in Chanhassen, Minnesota, and named it Paisley Park. The outside was white, but the inside was colorful and full of life. He had pet doves, walls painted to look like the sky, and purple velvet sofas.

Paisley Park was Prince's home, music studio, and concert venue. He wrote thousands of songs there, including the music for the 1989 film *Batman*, based on the TV show that had inspired Prince when he was a boy.

But Prince was frustrated. His deal with Warner Bros. gave the company control over what Prince could and couldn't do with his music. So, in 1993, Prince broke free. He changed his name to a symbol that couldn't be pronounced. He hoped that if his name wasn't Prince anymore, Warner Bros. couldn't tell him what to do. For seven years, people called him The Artist Formerly Known as Prince.

He took his power back and showed other artists how to speak up for themselves.

Prince also created work for children. He appeared on an episode of *Muppets Tonight* and sang with Kermit the Frog, Rizzo the Rat, and other Muppets. He wrote "The Song of the Heart" for *Happy Feet*, an animated movie about a penguin who wanted to be free to dance.

In 2007, Prince performed at the Super Bowl. It rained in the middle of his act, but nothing stopped Prince. He kept on playing, and the audience loved it! Many people consider it to be the best halftime show ever.

Prince's home became famous, too. His friends were always welcome at Paisley Park. Some made music in his studios. Prince also invited hundreds of people to concerts and donated the money he made to charities that helped people in need.

Prince won Grammy Awards, Black Entertainment Television (BET) Awards, American Music Awards, the BET Lifetime Achievement Award, and many others. In 2004, he was inducted into the Rock & Roll Hall of Fame.

On April 21, 2016, Prince died at Paisley Park, after he accidentally took too much of a prescription medication. The world was in shock. People came from all over to place flowers and candles outside Prince's home.

Today, Paisley Park is open to the public. Visitors can see his studios, instruments, clothes, and other memorabilia.

Prince will always be missed, but he continues to share his magnificent gift. New songs from his vault, where he stored his extra music, were released. He also left behind a reminder that it is important to be—and speak up for—yourself.